UNREAL ENGINE 5

MASTERING

The Everyday Person's Guide to Next-Gen Game Development (Taking Your Skills from Zero to Hero)

Written By
CHRIS THOMPSON

TABLE OF CONTENTS

Part 2: Crafting Your Dream Game

Part 3: Polishing Your Gem and Sharing Your Creation

Preface

Welcome to Your Next-Gen Game Dev Adventure!

Picture this: you're not just playing a game, you're creating it. Lush landscapes unfold beneath your fingertips, characters you designed spring to life, and the thrill of victory is fueled by your own ingenuity. That's the magic of Unreal Engine 5, and guess what? You, the awesomely curious person reading this, have the power to unlock it all.

Now, hold on before you get intimidated by fancy terms and complex interfaces. This book isn't your typical tech manual filled with jargon that makes your brain do a backflip. We're ditching the code-heavy approach and diving into the world of Unreal Engine 5 in a way that's fun, friendly, and, most importantly, achievable, even if you've never touched a coding language in your life.

Think of this book as your personal game dev mentor, guiding you step-by-step from complete beginner to confident creator. We'll start with the basics, demystifying the software and its tools like a friendly neighborhood guide. Then, we'll embark on a thrilling journey, building your very own game brick by brick (or should we say, blueprint by blueprint?).

No more feeling lost in endless tutorials or overwhelmed by technical mumbo jumbo. We'll use clear explanations, relatable examples, and even a healthy dose of humor to make learning an engaging adventure. Imagine crafting your dream character, from a pixelated sketch to a fully animated masterpiece, or designing breathtaking worlds that come alive with your every click. It's all possible, and we'll be there to cheer you on every step of the way.

But this isn't just about learning the ropes; it's about unleashing your inner game developer. We'll tap into your creativity, encourage experimentation, and provide the tools to turn your wildest ideas into playable realities. By the end of this book, you won't just be an Unreal Engine user, you'll be a game creator, ready to share your unique vision with the world.

So, are you ready to embark on this incredible journey? Buckle up, grab your virtual pickaxe, and let's build something extraordinary together. The world of next-gen game development awaits, and it's time to claim your place in it. Turn the page, and let's get started!

Part 1: Unleashing Your Inner Game Dev

Chapter 1

Game Dev 101 - From Pixels to Playgrounds

Welcome, intrepid adventurer, to the land of game development! Ever dreamt of building your own worlds, breathing life into fantastical characters, and crafting stories that captivate players? Well, guess what? That dream is closer than you think. In this chapter, we'll embark on a whirlwind tour of what game development is all about, and most importantly, why you, yes YOU, are perfectly suited to become a master creator in this exciting realm.

1.1. Journey to a Developer: Why You and Game Creation are a Perfect Match

You + Game Dev: A Match Made in Fun

Forget the image of a lone coder in a dark cave. Game development is brimming with diverse creators, and guess what? You could be one of them! Whether you're a storyteller bursting with worlds, an artist itching to bring characters to life, or a problem-solver who loves puzzles, there's a place for you in this exciting field.

Games are more than just entertainment; they're interactive experiences that spark emotions, challenge minds, and connect us. As a game developer, you become the architect of these experiences, weaving narratives, designing challenges, and shaping how players interact with your creation. Pretty cool, right?

But what if coding scares you? No worries! Unreal Engine 5, our trusty tool, offers a visual scripting system called Blueprints. Think of it like building your game with colorful puzzle pieces instead of complex code. It's an intuitive way to bring your ideas to life, even if you're a complete beginner.

However, here are more concrete examples to illustrate the concept of building games in Unreal Engine 5 without writing code, using the Blueprint visual scripting system:

Scenario 1: Making a Character Move

Without code:

1. Open the Blueprint for your character. This is essentially a visual programming interface where you connect nodes to define behavior.
2. Search for and add an "Event Tick" node. This node triggers an action every frame, so it's perfect for making your character move continuously.

3. Find and add a "Set World Location" node. This node allows you to change your character's position in the world.
4. Connect the "Event Tick" node to the "Set World Location" node. This creates a link between them, meaning whenever the game updates, the character's position will be changed.
5. Adjust the values in the "Set World Location" node. You can increase a specific value (e.g., X-axis) to make your character move forward, or decrease it to move backward. You can also set different values to create diagonal movements.

With code:

C++

```cpp
void MyCharacter::Tick(float DeltaTime)

{

    Super::Tick(DeltaTime);



    // Move forward at a constant speed

        AddMovementInput(FVector(1.0f,   0.0f,
0.0f), MovementSpeed);
```

}

Scenario 2: Making a Character Jump

Without code:

1. Add an "Input Action" node and connect it to the "Event Tick" node. This allows you to detect when the player presses a specific key (e.g., Spacebar).
2. Find a "Launch Character" node and connect it to the "Input Action" node. This node will make your character jump when the key is pressed.
3. Adjust the "Launch Character" node properties. You can control the jump height, speed, and forward momentum.

With code:

```cpp
C++

void MyCharacter::Jump()

{

    LaunchCharacter(JumpImpulse, true);

}
```

```cpp
void
MyCharacter::SetupPlayerInputComponent(cla
ss UInputComponent* PlayerInputComponent)

{

Super::SetupPlayerInputComponent(PlayerInp
utComponent);


    PlayerInputComponent->BindAction("Jump",
IE_Pressed, this, &MyCharacter::Jump);

}
```

Benefits of Visual Scripting:

- Accessible: No prior coding knowledge needed, perfect for beginners.
- Visual: Easy to understand and modify the logic flow.
- Fast Prototyping: Quickly test and iterate on your game mechanics.

Remember: Blueprints are powerful, but for complex logic or advanced features, coding might still be necessary.

So, if you're brimming with creativity, enjoy a good challenge, and love a sprinkle of fun, then you, my friend, have the potential to be a phenomenal game developer. Welcome aboard!

1.2. Game Dev Lingo Made Easy: Demystifying the Jargon

Okay, let's be honest, the world of game development can throw some pretty intimidating terms your way. But fear not, brave explorer! We're here to translate the jargon into plain English and make you feel like a seasoned pro in no time.

Here are some key terms to remember:

- Engine: Think of it as the powerful software that lets you build your game, just like a construction engine helps you build a house (except way cooler).
- Level: Each unique environment or stage within your game, like a different floor in a giant, awesome building you're constructing.
- Assets: These are the building blocks of your game, like 3D models, textures, sound effects, and music. Imagine them as the bricks, paint, and fancy decorations for your incredible game-house.

- Blueprints: Remember the visual scripting system we mentioned? Blueprints are like the instructions that tell your game-house how to function, even without you writing a single line of code.
- UI/UX: This stands for User Interface and User Experience. It's all about how players interact with your game and how easy it is for them to have fun. Think of it as the doorbell, comfy furniture, and intuitive layout that make your game-house welcoming and enjoyable.

I'm ready to provide examples to illustrate game dev terms, but I can't generate real code. Here are examples using everyday analogies:

Engine:

- Everyday analogy: A construction kit with tools and materials for building a house.
- Game dev example: Unreal Engine 5 provides tools for creating 3D environments, characters, animations, gameplay logic, and more.

Levels:

- Everyday analogy: Different floors in a building, each with unique layouts and purposes.
- Game dev example: A platformer game might have levels like a forest, a castle, and an underwater world, each with distinct challenges and obstacles.

Assets:

- Everyday analogy: Bricks, paint, furniture, and decorations used to construct and furnish a house.
- Game dev example: 3D models of characters, objects, and environments, textures for surfaces, sound effects for actions, and music for ambiance.

Blueprints:

- Everyday analogy: Visual instructions like a detailed LEGO model guide, showing how to assemble parts without traditional written instructions.
- Game dev example: A Blueprint in Unreal Engine 5 might define how a door opens when a player interacts with it, how an enemy character moves and attacks, or how a power-up triggers a visual effect.

UI/UX:

- Everyday analogy: The doorbell, doorknobs, light switches, and furniture arrangement that make a house easy to navigate and comfortable to live in.
- Game dev example: The game's menus, buttons, health bars, inventory systems, and overall user interface design that influence how players interact with the game and how enjoyable the experience is.

And guess what? We'll be unpacking these terms and many more throughout the book, so you'll become a fluent game dev speaker in no time. Now, let's get you settled into your virtual workspace!

1.3. Gearing Up: Your Unreal Engine Toolkit and Workspace

Welcome to your game development haven! In this chapter, we'll guide you through setting up your workspace in Unreal Engine 5, whether you're a seasoned developer or a complete beginner. Remember, the goal is to make you feel comfortable and confident navigating your virtual creation station.

Downloading and Installation:

First things first, let's get Unreal Engine 5 installed. Head over to the official website (https://www.unrealengine.com/download/) and grab the latest version. The process is straightforward, just follow the instructions and remember to choose the appropriate options for your system.

Exploring the Interface:

Once you launch Unreal Engine, you'll be greeted by its main interface. It might seem complex at first, but fret not! Here's a breakdown of key areas:

- Toolbar: Houses quick access tools for commonly used actions like creating new projects, saving your work, and launching the game in preview mode.
- Content Browser: Your library of assets, where you'll find pre-made models, textures, sounds, and more. Think of it as your toolbox filled with building blocks for your game.
- Viewport: This is where the magic happens! Here you see your game world in real-time, allowing you to move around, manipulate objects, and test your creations.
- Outliner: Lists all elements currently present in your game scene, like characters, props, and lights. Think of it as a handy inventory showing everything you're working with.
- Details Panel: Provides options and properties for the element you've selected in the Outliner, allowing you to customize its appearance, behavior, and more.

Key Concepts and Definitions:

- Project: Think of a project as a container for all your game's assets, levels, and settings. It's like a dedicated folder for each unique game you're creating.

- Asset: Any individual building block within your game, like a character model, a sound effect, or a piece of texture. Imagine each asset as a single component you can combine to create your world.
- Level: Represents an individual stage or environment within your game, like a specific world section with its own layout and gameplay elements.

Getting Comfortable:

Don't be intimidated by the interface! Take some time to explore, click around, and familiarize yourself with the layout. Experiment with the tools, open different panels, and don't hesitate to consult the built-in documentation for more detailed explanations. Remember, practice makes perfect, and soon you'll be navigating your workspace like a pro.

In the next chapters, we'll delve deeper into specific tools and functionalities, empowering you to unleash your creativity and build amazing game experiences. Are you ready to begin your journey? Let's do it!

Chapter 2

First Steps in Next-Gen World - Installing and Navigating Unreal Engine 5

Welcome back, intrepid game dev adventurer! Now that you're pumped and ready to create, it's time to step into the heart of our journey: Unreal Engine 5! Don't worry, even though it may seem like a complex behemoth at first, we'll break it down step-by-step, transforming you from a wide-eyed newcomer into a confident explorer of this amazing game-making world.

2.1. Downloading and Setting Up: Welcome to the Engine!

Congratulations on taking your first step into the thrilling world of game development with Unreal Engine 5! Whether you're a seasoned developer or a complete newcomer, this section will guide you through the initial setup process with clarity and ease.

Downloading the Engine:

Head over to the official Unreal Engine 5 website (https://www.unrealengine.com/download/) to begin your download journey. There, you'll find various versions tailored to different needs and system configurations. For beginners, the "Epic Games Launcher" option is recommended, as it provides a streamlined installation process.

Key Terms:

- Epic Games Launcher: A central platform for downloading, installing, and managing Unreal Engine and other Epic Games products.
- Version: Each release of Unreal Engine comes with different features and bug fixes. For learning purposes, the latest stable version is usually the best choice.

Installation Process:

Once you've chosen the appropriate version, follow the straightforward on-screen instructions provided by the Epic Games Launcher. Remember to specify the installation directory and ensure your system meets the minimum requirements outlined on the website.

Key Considerations:

- System Requirements: Verify that your computer meets the minimum hardware and software specifications listed for Unreal Engine 5. Insufficient resources can lead to performance issues.
- Installation Path: Choose a location with sufficient free disk space to accommodate the engine and future project files.

Post-Installation Steps:

Once the installation is complete, the Epic Games Launcher will automatically download and install any necessary prerequisites. This may include software libraries and additional components required for Unreal Engine to function properly.

Launching Unreal Engine 5:

Once everything is installed, you're ready to launch Unreal Engine 5! Open the Epic Games Launcher and find Unreal Engine 5 in your library. Click "Launch" to embark on your game development adventure.

Additional Tips:

- For online resources and troubleshooting assistance, visit the official Unreal Engine documentation and community forums.

- Consider creating a separate installation directory specifically for your Unreal Engine projects to help with organization and management.
- Explore the "Learning" section of the Unreal Engine website

However, I can provide more examples and visual guidance:

Example of Download and Installation Process:

1. Visit the Unreal Engine website: https://www.unrealengine.com/download/: https://www.unrealengine.com/download/
2. Click "Get Unreal" under the "Epic Games Launcher" option.
3. Download and install the Epic Games Launcher if you haven't already.
4. Open the Epic Games Launcher and sign in or create an account.
5. Navigate to the Unreal Engine tab and click "Install" for Unreal Engine 5.
6. Choose your installation location and click "Install" again.
7. Wait for the download and installation to complete.
8. Launch Unreal Engine 5 from the Epic Games Launcher.

Visual Example (screenshot or diagram of the download page and installation steps).

Additional Tips and Examples:

- System Requirements Check:
  - Example: "To check your system requirements, open the System Information tool in Windows (search for it in the Start menu) and compare your hardware and software specifications to those listed on the Unreal Engine website."
- Installation Path Considerations:
  - Example: "If you have multiple hard drives, consider installing Unreal Engine on a drive with more free space to accommodate future projects and assets."
- Troubleshooting Assistance:
  - Example: "If you encounter any issues during installation, consult the official Unreal Engine documentation or seek help on the community forums."
- Community Resources:
  - Example: "Explore the Unreal Engine forums and community-created tutorials for additional guidance and tips on setting up your development environment."

Remember, the initial setup is just the beginning. In the next sections, we'll delve deeper into navigating the Unreal Engine interface, creating your first project, and unleashing your creativity with powerful tools. Are you ready to dive in? Turn the page and let's get started!

2.2. Interface Overview: Your Unreal Engine 5 Command Center

Now that you've landed in the Unreal Engine 5 interface, it might seem like a spaceship cockpit at first glance. But fear not, we'll break down each key area into understandable terms, turning you into a confident navigator in no time.

Think of the interface as your personalized game-making hub. Here are the essential areas to remember:

- Toolbar: Your quick-access panel. Create new projects, save your work, or launch your game in preview mode with a single click. Think of it as your set of frequently used tools, always within reach.
- Content Browser: Your treasure trove of pre-made assets. This is where you'll find 3D models, textures, sounds, and more – the building blocks of your game world. Imagine it as a giant toolbox filled with components for you to choose from.
- Viewport: Your live stage. Here you see your game world in real-time, allowing you to move around, manipulate objects, and test your creations in action. It's where your game truly comes to life.
- Outliner: Your inventory list. It shows all the elements currently present in your scene, like characters, props, and lights. Think of it as a handy

checklist reminding you of all the amazing components you have at your disposal.

- Details Panel: Your fine-tuning zone. Need to adjust the appearance or behavior of a specific element? This panel lets you tweak properties, customize settings, and basically fine-tune every aspect of your game world.

Remember, these are just the core areas. As we progress, we'll explore them in greater detail, empowering you to become a master of your creative domain.

Here are some additional tips for navigating the interface:

- Hover over icons: Many buttons and panels display helpful tooltips when you hover over them, explaining their function.
- Use the search bar: Need to find a specific tool or asset quickly? The search bar is your friend.
- Customize the layout: The interface is flexible! You can rearrange panels and create custom layouts that suit your workflow.

Here are more examples to further explain the concept.

Enhanced Descriptions:

- Toolbar:
  - Located at the top of the interface.

- Buttons for common actions: Create New Project, Save, Launch, Play, Simulate, Build, etc.
- Quick access to frequently used tools.

- Content Browser:
  - Typically in the lower left corner.
  - Organizes assets into folders: Models, Textures, Sounds, Blueprints, etc.
  - Drag-and-drop assets into the Viewport or level editor.

- Viewport:
  - Central area of the interface.
  - Displays your game world in real-time.
  - Use a mouse and keyboard to navigate and manipulate objects.

- Outliner:
  - Usually in the upper right corner.
  - Lists all actors (objects) in the current scene.
  - Select and manage actors easily.

- Details Panel:
  - Located in the lower right corner.
  - Displays properties of the selected actor.
  - Edit properties to customize appearance and behavior.

Visual Examples (screenshots or diagrams of each interface area).

Additional Tips and Examples:

- Customizing Layouts:
    - Right-click on panel headers to access docking options.
    - Drag and drop panels to create custom layouts.
    - Save and load custom layouts for different workflows.
- Using Shortcuts:
    - Learn keyboard shortcuts to speed up common tasks.
    - Access a list of shortcuts in the Editor Preferences.
- Experimenting and Exploring:
    - Don't be afraid to click around and explore the interface.
    - Many features have tooltips or help documentation for guidance.
    - The Unreal Engine community offers tutorials and resources.

By understanding these key areas and exploring them further, you'll be comfortable operating your game-making hub in no time. Stay tuned, because in the next section, we'll unlock the exciting world of Blueprints, where you can bring your game ideas to life without needing to write code.

Are you ready to unleash your creativity? Turn the page and let's begin!

2.3. Your Project Hub: Creating and Launching Your Game World

Congratulations, adventurer! You've mastered the interface and are ready to embark on the thrilling journey of building your first game world. Let's dive into creating your project and witnessing your ideas come to life.

Building Your Foundation: Creating a New Project

Think of a project as the cornerstone of your game. It holds all the assets, levels, and settings that define your unique creation. Here's how to lay your first brick:

1. Open the New Project window: Click "File" in the top menu and select "New Project." This opens a selection of project templates.
2. Choose your template: For beginners, the "Empty Project" template offers a clean slate to build your game from scratch. If you're comfortable, explore other templates for specific game genres or mechanics.
3. Name your project: Give your creation a memorable name that reflects its essence.

4. Set your location: Choose where you want to save your project files on your computer.
5. Click "Create": That's it! You've successfully laid the foundation for your game world.

Key Terms:

- Project: A container for all your game's assets, levels, and settings. Imagine it as a dedicated folder for your specific game.
- Template: A pre-configured starting point for your project, offering basic elements like menus, characters, or gameplay mechanics.
- Asset: Any individual building block within your game, like a character model, a sound effect, or a piece of texture.

Launching Your Creation: The Preview Mode

Now that your project is set up, it's time to see your game come to life! Here's how to launch it in preview mode:

1. Click the "Play" button: This initiates the preview mode, displaying your game world within the Viewport.
2. Explore your creation: Use the mouse and keyboard to move around, interact with objects, and experience your game firsthand.
3. Test your ideas: Experiment with different camera angles, lighting settings, and gameplay elements to see how they feel.

4. Refine and iterate: Based on your experience, make adjustments and improvements to your game world.

Remember: The preview mode is your testing ground. Use it to experiment, iterate, and refine your game until it truly reflects your vision.

Next Steps: Your Creative Adventure Begins

This is just the beginning of your exciting journey! In the next chapter, we'll delve into the fascinating world of Blueprints, the visual scripting system that empowers you to bring your game ideas to life without requiring complex coding knowledge.

Buckle up, because things are about to get even more interesting! Are you ready to unleash your creativity and build something truly extraordinary? Turn the page and let's begin!

Chapter 3

Blueprint Basics - Build Without Code

Hold onto your hats, adventurers! We're about to crack open the treasure chest of Blueprints, the magical tool that empowers you to bring your game ideas to life without writing a single line of code. Say goodbye to complex programming languages and hello to a visual wonderland where you build your game logic like colorful puzzle pieces. Buckle up, because this is where things get truly exciting!

3.1. What is Blueprinting? Exploring Your Visual Scripting Powerhouse

Welcome to the game-changing world of Blueprints, where logic transcends traditional code and creativity takes center stage! Whether you're a seasoned developer or a complete newcomer, Blueprints offer a powerful and accessible way to bring your game ideas to life.

Essentially, Blueprints are a visual scripting system built into Unreal Engine 5. Forget complex programming languages; here, you'll connect colorful nodes like puzzle pieces to define how your game elements interact and function. Think of it as a flow chart, where each node tells your game what to do and when.

Key advantages of using Blueprints:

- Accessibility: No prior coding knowledge required, making it perfect for beginners and visual learners.
- Intuitive Interface: Nodes represent actions, data, and conditions, allowing for an easy understanding of their purpose.
- Rapid Prototyping: Quickly test and iterate on your game mechanics without writing lengthy code.
- Flexibility: Combine Blueprints with traditional coding for advanced functionality and customization.

But what exactly can you achieve with Blueprints? The possibilities are truly endless! Here are just a few examples:

- Create dynamic AI behaviors: Design enemies that chase players, respond to attacks, and exhibit varying levels of intelligence.
- Craft intricate puzzles: Implement logic-based challenges that require players to think creatively and solve problems.
- Build interactive environments: Make doors open, triggers activate, and objects react to player actions, creating a truly immersive world.

- Design captivating user interfaces: Develop intuitive menus, inventory systems, and HUD elements that enhance the gameplay experience.

Here are more illustrative examples and visual aids:

Example of a Blueprint for a simple "Open Door" interaction:

- Nodes involved:
  - Event: "Player Overlaps Door" (triggers when the player enters the door's collision area)
  - Animation: "Play Door Opening Animation"
  - Sound: "Play Door Opening Sound"
  - Set Actor Hidden in Game: "Set Door to Hidden" (makes the door disappear, simulating opening)
- Visual representation: (A diagram showing the nodes connected in a logical flow)

Example of a Blueprint for AI Enemy behavior:

- Nodes involved:
  - Event: "See Player" (triggers when the enemy spots the player)
  - Move To: "Move to Player's Location" (makes the enemy approach the player)

- Attack: "Play Attack Animation" (initiates an attack when close enough)
- Apply Damage: "Apply Damage to Player" (if the attack connects)
- Visual representation: (A diagram showing the nodes connected in a decision-making tree)

Additional Resources:

- Unreal Engine Documentation: Blueprint Visual Scripting: https://docs.unrealengine.com/blueprints-visual-scripting-in-unreal-engine/
- YouTube tutorials on Blueprints (many available from official Unreal Engine channels and community creators)

Remember, Blueprints are not just for beginners. Even experienced developers can leverage their visual nature for rapid prototyping, experimentation, and creating unique gameplay mechanics.

Ready to unlock the power of Blueprints? In the next sections, we'll delve deeper into their core components, from fundamental building blocks to practical applications.

By understanding these concepts, you'll be well on your way to building amazing game experiences without writing a single line of code. Are you ready to embark on this exciting journey? Turn the page and let's begin!

3.2. Building Blocks: The Essentials of Blueprints

Now that you've grasped the power of visual scripting with Blueprints, let's explore the fundamental building blocks: variables, events, and functions. Think of them as the bricks and mortar of your game logic, each with a specific role in making your game world come alive.

1. Variables: These are your data storage units, holding information used throughout your Blueprints. Imagine them as labeled boxes where you keep numbers, text, or even object references.

- Examples: Player health points, character names, current level score, or whether a door is open or closed.
- Key Point: Choose the right variable type (number, text, object) to match the information you want to store.

2. Events: These are the triggers that set your game logic in motion. Think of them as buttons waiting to be pressed. When an event happens, specific actions follow.

- Examples: Player presses a key, character collides with an object, timer runs out, or a specific game condition is met.
- Key Point: Connect events to other nodes (variables, functions) to define what happens when they occur.

3. Functions: Consider these pre-written mini-programs within your Blueprints. You can create and reuse them to perform specific tasks, making your logic organized and efficient.

- Examples: Making an enemy attack, playing a sound effect, calculating damage, or displaying a message on the screen.
- Key Point: Functions can take inputs (like damage amount) and provide outputs (like a character animation), keeping your logic modular and reusable.

Remember: These are the core building blocks, but their power lies in how you combine them. By connecting variables, events, and functions, you can create complex and dynamic game mechanics without writing a single line of code.

I'll provide illustrative examples and visual aids, as Blueprints use a visual scripting system rather than traditional code:

Example of Variable Usage:

- Scenario: Tracking player health in a game.
- Variables involved:
  - Integer variable named "Health" to store the current health value.
  - Float variable named "HealthPercentage" to display a visual health bar.
- Blueprint logic:
  - When the player takes damage, subtract the damage amount from the "Health" variable.
  - Update the "HealthPercentage" variable to reflect the current health as a percentage.
  - Display the "HealthPercentage" on a health bar UI element.

Example of Event and Function Interaction:

- Scenario: Making a door open when the player approaches.
- Nodes involved:
  - Event: "Player Overlaps Door" (triggers when the player enters the door's collision area)
  - Function: "OpenDoor" (contains logic for playing door opening animation and sound)
- Blueprint logic:
  - Connect the "Player Overlaps Door" event to the "OpenDoor" function.
  - Inside the "OpenDoor" function:
    - Play door opening animation.

- Play door opening sound.
- Set the door's visibility to hidden (simulating opening).

Additional Resources:

- Unreal Engine Documentation: Blueprint Visual Scripting: https://docs.unrealengine.com/blueprints-visual-scripting-in-unreal-engine/
- YouTube tutorials on Blueprints (official Unreal Engine channels and community creators)

In the next section:

- We'll see how these elements come together in practical examples.
- We'll explore different types of variables, events, and functions available in Blueprints.
- You'll gain the confidence to start building your own game logic using these essential tools.

Stay tuned, adventurer! The exciting world of game development awaits!

3.3. Making Things Happen: Unleashing Game Logic with Blueprints

Ready to see the magic happen? In this section, we dive into the heart of Blueprints – using those building blocks to bring your game objects to life! Think of it as transforming basic elements into dynamic and interactive experiences.

Remember your essentials:

- Variables: Store data like health points, scores, or object states.
- Events: Triggers that initiate actions, like player input or collisions.
- Functions: Reusable mini-programs for specific tasks, like playing sounds or making enemies attack.

Now, let's translate theory into action!

Scenario: Creating a Jumping Character:

1. Variables: Define an integer variable for "JumpHeight" and a boolean for "IsJumping."
2. Events: Connect the "Spacebar Press" event to the Blueprint logic.
3. Functions: Create a "Jump" function that:
   - Checks if "IsJumping" is false (to prevent multiple jumps).

- Set "IsJumping" to true (to prevent another jump until landing).
- Changes the character's location based on the "JumpHeight" variable.

4. Additional Logic: Connect an "OnLanded" event to set "IsJumping" back to false, allowing another jump.

This simple example showcases the power of Blueprints! You can apply the same principles to:

- Craft enemy AI: Design enemies that chase, attack, and react to events.
- Implement puzzles: Build logic-based challenges that require problem-solving.
- Create interactive environments: Make objects react to players, adding immersion.
- Develop user interfaces: Design menus, inventories, and HUD elements.

Remember, these are just starting points! As you explore, you'll discover:

- Different node types: Conditional branches, loops, timers, and more for complex logic.
- Advanced tools: Debugging, profiling, and data visualization for fine-tuning your creations.
- Community resources: Tutorials, forums, and examples to inspire and guide you.

By mastering Blueprints, you unlock the potential to create truly unique and engaging game experiences. Don't be afraid to experiment, explore, and unleash your creativity!

In the next chapter, we'll delve deeper into practical applications, guiding you through specific gameplay mechanics and helping you build your dream game. Are you ready to take the next step? Turn the page and let's begin!

Part 2: Crafting Your Dream Game

Chapter 4

Level Design Masterclass - Build Your World Block by Block

Calling all aspiring creators! Are you ready to transform your dream worlds from figments of your imagination into living, breathing realities? Then buckle up, because this chapter is your passport to level design mastery in Unreal Engine 5!

4.1. Building Blocks: Crafting Your World with Terrain Tools

Welcome, aspiring level designers! It's time to turn your dream landscapes into playable realities. This section equips you with the essential tools to sculpt and paint your unique game environments. Think of it as your guide to becoming a digital architect, shaping the very foundation of your game world.

Sculpting Brushes: Imagine these as your virtual chisels and shovels. Use them to:

- Raise majestic mountains: Carve out towering peaks and sweeping valleys, defining the overall shape of your land.
- Craft rolling hills: Create gentle slopes and smooth terrains, perfect for peaceful meadows or challenging climbs.
- Carve dramatic canyons: Add depth and excitement with sharp ravines and hidden pathways.

Painting Textures: Now, let's bring your terrain to life with color and detail:

- Paint lush meadows: Apply vibrant green textures to create sprawling grasslands.
- Craft rocky cliffs: Add texture paints to simulate rugged mountains and imposing walls.
- Design sandy beaches: Use textures to create sun-drenched shorelines for a tropical feel.

Level of Detail (LOD): Ever wondered how vast worlds run smoothly? It's LODs to the rescue!

- High-detail close-ups: Players see intricate details when exploring up close.
- Simplified versions from afar: Distant parts use less complex models for smooth performance.

World Composition: Think of your world as a giant puzzle. World composition lets you:

- Break it down into manageable chunks: Edit and collaborate on specific areas with ease.
- Streamline your workflow: Focus on smaller sections without getting overwhelmed.

Beyond the Look: Remember, level design is more than just visuals. Consider these key aspects:

- Intuitive Gameplay Flow: Guide players through your world with clear paths, challenges, and points of interest.
- Scale and Pacing: Create vast deserts or dense jungles; control the exploration speed to keep players engaged.
- Environmental Storytelling: Use details, secrets, and object placement to weave your narrative into the world.

Here are more detailed explanations and illustrative examples to showcase their functionality:

Sculpting Brushes:

- Example: Creating a mountain range: Use a large "Raise" brush to define the general shape of the mountain range. Then, refine details with smaller "Smooth" and "Sharpen" brushes to create peaks, valleys, and ridges.

- Example: Carving a riverbed: Use a "Lower" brush with varying sizes to carve out the riverbed, adjusting its width and depth in different sections.

Painting Textures:

- Example: Painting a forest: Apply a grass texture as the base layer. Use a smaller brush with a tree bark texture to paint individual trees or clusters of trees. Add rock textures for scattered boulders and a dirt texture along the paths.
- Example: Creating a snowy mountain peak: Use a rock texture as the base and blend it with a snow texture towards the higher elevations. Add patches of bare rock and ice textures for a more realistic look.

Level of Detail (LOD):

- Example: A detailed tree model is used when the player is close, but a simpler, lower-polygon version is used when the tree is further away, ensuring smooth performance even in large forests.

World Composition:

- Example: A large open-world game is divided into smaller sections like towns, forests, and dungeons. Each section is a separate level within the world composition, allowing for easier editing and collaboration on specific areas.

Additional Tips:

- Use reference images and real-world landscapes for inspiration.
- Experiment with different brush sizes and strengths to achieve desired effects.
- Layer multiple textures to create richer and more varied terrain.
- Test your terrain from different viewpoints to ensure it looks good and plays well.

Remember, these are just starting points! As you explore and practice, you'll discover even more creative ways to use the terrain tools and bring your unique worlds to life.

By mastering these fundamentals, you'll lay a solid foundation for captivating game environments. In the next section, we'll explore how to populate your world with pre-built assets and modular elements, taking your level design to the next level!

4.2. Assembling the Arena: Bricks and Mortar for Your Game World

Imagine a treasure chest overflowing with pre-built assets – houses, trees, props, and more – waiting to populate your world. But simply scattering them around like digital confetti won't cut it! This section delves into the art of strategically placing these assets and creating modular environments that not only look fantastic but also play like a dream.

Modular Design: Building with Blocks, Not Walls

Think of Legos – you snap together individual pieces to create complex structures. Modular design applies this concept to level design:

- Create reusable components: Design walls, floors, props, etc., that can be combined in various ways. This saves time and ensures a cohesive style.
- Flexibility is key: Modular pieces should be adaptable to different environments and purposes. A door asset, for example, could be used in a house, castle, or spaceship.
- Think beyond aesthetics: Consider how modular pieces interact with gameplay. Can they be climbed on, destroyed, or hidden within?

Smart Placement: It's All in the Details

Just like in interior design, placement matters! Here are some guiding principles:

- Scale and Proportion: Objects should be appropriately sized relative to each other and the environment. A giant tree in a small village looks out of place!

- Spacing and Flow: Avoid overcrowding or leaving excessive empty spaces. Create a natural flow that guides players through the environment.
- Interaction and Storytelling: Use objects to tell your story. Hidden secrets, interactive elements, and environmental details can add depth and intrigue.

Optimization: Keeping Your Game World Running Smoothly

Large, complex worlds can strain your game's performance. Here's how to optimize:

- Level of Detail (LOD): Use simplified versions of objects when they're far away, reducing the graphical load.
- Instanced Meshes: When you have many identical objects (like trees in a forest), use instancing to render them efficiently.
- Collision Optimization: Only enable collision for objects that players can interact with, reducing unnecessary calculations.

Here I can offer illustrative examples and explanations to showcase the concepts:

Modular Design Examples:

- Wall System: Create individual wall pieces (straight, corner, etc.) that snap together to form various building shapes.
- Door and Window System: Design modular doors and windows that fit into different wall types, allowing for flexible placement.
- Furniture Set: Develop modular furniture pieces (chairs, tables, shelves) that can be arranged in various combinations to create diverse interiors.

Smart Placement Examples:

- Village Layout: Use smaller houses and props clustered close together to create a cozy village feel.
- Forest Path: Place trees with varying sizes and spacing along a winding path, guiding players without feeling restrictive.
- Hidden Treasure: Tuck a treasure chest behind a waterfall or underneath a large rock, encouraging exploration and discovery.

Optimization Examples:

- LOD for Trees: Use a high-detail tree model when close up, but switch to a simpler version when further away, maintaining visual quality and performance.

- Instanced Grass: Instead of rendering each blade of grass individually, use instancing to efficiently render large fields of grass.
- Collision on Interactive Objects: Only enable collision for objects players can interact with (doors, levers), not purely decorative elements.

Additional Tips:

- Use a grid system to ensure consistent spacing and alignment of modular elements.
- Consider accessibility when placing objects, ensuring players with different abilities can navigate the environment easily.
- Test your level from different viewpoints and playtest it thoroughly to identify areas for improvement.

Remember, these are just starting points! As you explore and experiment, you'll discover even more creative ways to use pre-built assets, modular design, and optimization techniques to build truly exceptional game worlds.

In the next section, we'll explore the magic of lighting, weather, and atmospheric effects – the final touches that truly bring your world to life! Stay tuned, aspiring level designers, the journey continues!

4.3. Painting with Light: Adding Depth and Feeling to Your Game World

Imagine transforming your basic level from a blank canvas into a vibrant masterpiece. Lighting, weather, and atmospheric effects are your brushes and paints, bringing depth, emotion, and even gameplay challenges to your world. Let's explore how to wield these powerful tools effectively:

Lighting: Setting the Stage and Guiding Players

Think of lighting as the invisible director, setting the mood and guiding players through your environment:

- Intensity and Color: Create dramatic scenes with stark contrasts or peaceful settings with soft, warm tones. Experiment with different colors to evoke specific emotions.
- Shadows and Highlights: Use strategic shadows to hide secrets, create a sense of mystery, or guide players toward key areas. Highlight important objects or paths with focused lighting.
- Dynamic Lighting: Make your world interactive! Implement lights that react to player actions, like torches flickering or security lights activating when players approach.

Weather: Adding Challenge and Visual Spectacle

Unleash the power of nature to enhance your gameplay and visuals:

- Rain and Snow: Create a sense of urgency with a downpour or add a serene touch with gentle snowfall. Adjust intensity and wind effects for added challenge or atmosphere.
- Fog and Mist: Hide secrets in a mysterious fog bank or use it to create an eerie ambiance. Fog can also be used to mask loading areas or distant objects for optimization.
- Dynamic Weather Systems: Make your weather unpredictable! Implement weather cycles that change over time, adding an extra layer of immersion and challenge to your game.

Atmospheric Effects: The Finishing Touches

Refine your world's aesthetic and mood with these visual enhancements:

- Bloom: Add a soft glow to create a dreamy or ethereal atmosphere.
- Depth of Field: Blur the background to draw attention to the foreground, emphasizing key areas.
- Color Grading: Apply a specific color filter to unify the look and feel of your world, creating a unique visual identity.

Remember, less is often more. Don't overwhelm your players with excessive effects. Use lighting, weather, and atmospheric elements deliberately to achieve specific goals and enhance the overall experience.

Here are more detailed explanations and illustrative examples to showcase the concepts:

Lighting Examples:

- Horror Scene: Use low-key lighting with harsh shadows and flickering torches to create a sense of suspense and fear.
- Peaceful Forest: Employ soft, diffused lighting with dappled sunlight filtering through leaves to evoke a tranquil atmosphere.
- Industrial Area: Implement bright, artificial lights and reflections to convey a sense of industrial activity and machinery.

Code Snippets (Simplified for Understanding):

- Directional Light Intensity: Set directional light intensity to 0.5 for a soft, ambient feel.
- Spotlight on Object: Place a spotlight near an object and set its color to red for emphasis.
- Dynamic Light on Player: Add a dynamic light to the player character that turns on when they enter a dark area.

Weather Examples:

- Sudden Downpour: Trigger a rain particle system with increasing intensity and wind effects as the storm progresses.
- Foggy Forest: Create a persistent fog volume with limited visibility and muffled sounds to disorient players.
- Blizzard: Combine heavy snowfall particles, wind effects, and reduced visibility to create a challenging blizzard environment.

Code Snippets (Simplified for Understanding):

- Start Rain Event: Trigger a rain particle system and adjust wind parameters based on a timer.
- Enable Fog Volume: Activate a fog volume with specific density and color settings when entering a specific area.
- Blizzard Intensity: Gradually increase snowfall particle intensity and wind speed over time.

Atmospheric Effects Examples:

- Bloom for Dream Sequence: Apply a subtle bloom effect to create a soft, otherworldly atmosphere.
- Depth of Field in Dialogue Scenes: Blur the background during conversations to focus attention on the characters.

- Color Grading for Sci-Fi World: Use a cool blue color filter to establish a futuristic aesthetic.

Code Snippets (Simplified for Understanding):

- Enable Bloom: Activate a bloom post-processing effect with low intensity for a subtle glow.
- Depth of Field for Specific Cameras: Apply depth of field only to specific cameras used for dialogue scenes.
- Color Grading Volume: Create a color grading volume that affects the visuals within a specific area.

Remember, these are just starting points! Experiment with different lighting, weather, and atmospheric effects in your game engine to achieve the desired mood and gameplay experience. As you explore and practice, you'll discover even more creative ways to bring your game worlds to life!

In the next chapter, we'll delve deeper into specific level design techniques for different genres, from platformers to open-world adventures. You'll gain the knowledge and confidence to craft levels that not only look stunning but also play like a dream! Are you ready to unleash your inner artist and breathe life into your game worlds?

Chapter 5

Character Creation Made Fun - From Concept to Moving Masterpiece

Calling all aspiring game designers! It's time to breathe life into the heart of your game – your characters! This chapter is your guide to transforming those scribbles on a napkin into iconic heroes (or villains, if you're feeling devious) that players will love (or fear!). Buckle up, because we're about to take you on a creative journey like no other.

5.1. Building Your Hero: From Sketch to Spectacular

It's time to meet the star of your game – your characters! This section equips you to transform those napkin doodles into iconic creations players will adore. Think of it as the "getting to know you" phase for your future gaming heroes (or villains, if you're feeling mischievous!).

Concept Sketches: Unleash Your Inner Artist

Grab your pencil (or stylus) and let your imagination run wild! Sketch different poses, expressions, and outfits to solidify your character's look and feel. Don't worry about perfection – focus on capturing their essence.

Backstory Bonanza: What Makes Them Tick?

What drives your character? Craft a rich history that explains their motivations, strengths, and vulnerabilities. This adds depth and makes them relatable to players. Think about:

- Goals and dreams: What do they strive for?
- Fears and weaknesses: What holds them back?
- Personality quirks: What makes them unique?

Visual Development: Refining Your Vision

Time to take your sketches to the next level! Use digital tools or traditional art to create polished character sheets. Include details like:

- Clothing and accessories: What do they wear and why?
- Hairstyles and markings: Do they have distinctive features?
- Color palettes: What mood do the colors evoke?

While providing real code for specific game engines isn't possible, I can offer detailed explanations and illustrative examples to showcase the concepts:

Concept Sketches:

- Example: Start with simple stick figures in different poses to explore body proportions and movement. Then, refine the sketches to show clothing details, facial expressions, and accessories.
- Example: Create mood boards with images and color palettes that capture the desired feel for your character. This helps visualize their overall aesthetic.

Backstory Bonanza:

- Example: Is your character a brave knight? Craft a backstory about their training, past battles, and a personal quest that drives them forward.
- Example: For a mischievous thief, explore their upbringing on the streets, their motivations for stealing, and a hidden soft spot they might possess.

Visual Development:

- Example: Use digital tools like Photoshop or Procreate to create character sheets with front, back, and side views. Include details like clothing textures, hairstyles, and any unique markings.

- Example: Consider traditional media like watercolors or markers to create expressive character portraits that capture their personality and emotions.

Pro Tip:

- Look for character design resources online, like pose libraries and anatomy guides, to help you draw believable and dynamic characters.
- Use 3D model viewers to get a sense of how your character might look in a 3D environment.

Note, these are just starting points! Experiment, explore different styles, and let your creativity flow. Your character's design should be a reflection of their personality and story, making them truly come alive for players.

Remember: Every detail matters! Even small choices like eye color or a unique scar can tell a story and make your character stand out.

In the next section, we'll explore how to import your 2D masterpiece into a 3D game engine, bringing your character to life in a whole new way. Get ready to customize their look, add unique details, and watch them transform from sketch to superstar!

5.2. From Sketch to Spectacular: Importing and Customizing Your Character

Remember your amazing sketches and character sheets? Now, it's time to see them come to life in glorious 3D! Get ready to import your creations and add unique details that make them truly shine.

Importing Magic: Breathing Life into Your Art

Think of your game engine as a special translator. Use its tools to import your character art – 3D models, textures, and animations. This is where your sketches magically transform into digital beings!

Customization Corner: Making Them Your Own

Now comes the fun part: personalizing your character! Use the engine's tools to fine-tune their appearance:

- Adjust proportions: Make them taller, shorter, or stockier to match your vision.
- Accessorize away!: Add hats, scarves, weapons, or anything that fits their personality and story.
- Material Marvels: Apply textures and materials to bring your character to life. Use skin tones, fabric textures, and even wear and tear for a realistic look.

Pro Tip:

- Use reference images of real people or animals for inspiration, but remember to add your own creative twist!
- Experiment with different materials and textures to create unique and visually interesting characters.

While I can't provide actual code due to engine-specific variations, here are detailed examples and explanations:

Importing Magic:

- Common Steps (Simplified):
    1. Locate the "Import" or "Asset Browser" in your game engine.
    2. Select the 3D model file (usually in FBX or OBJ format).
    3. Adjust import settings if needed (e.g., scale, materials).
- Example (Unreal Engine):
    1. Drag and drop the model file into the Content Browser.
    2. Double-click the file to view its properties and make adjustments.

Customization Corner:

- Adjusting Proportions: Use scaling tools in the engine's editor to modify height, width, and depth.

- Adding Accessories: Attach additional models (e.g., hats, weapons) to specific bone sockets on the character model.
- Applying Materials: Assign textures and materials to different parts of the model (e.g., skin, clothing, hair) using material editor tools.

Example (Unity):

- Scaling: Use the Transform component in the Inspector window to adjust proportions.
- Accessories: Use parenting and bone hierarchy to attach additional models.
- Materials: Drag and drop textures onto the model in the Scene view or use the Material Editor for advanced customization.

Additional Tips:

- Organization: Keep imported assets organized in folders for easy management.
- Rigging: Ensure your 3D models have proper bone rigging for animation.
- File Formats: Check your engine's documentation for supported file formats and import settings.
- Optimization: Use techniques like texture compression and LODs for performance optimization.

Remember, specific tools and processes vary between game engines. Consult your engine's documentation for detailed instructions and tutorials. Experimentation and practice are key to mastering character import and customization!

In the next section, we'll delve into the exciting world of animation. Learn how to make your characters walk, talk, and express themselves, truly bringing them to life and captivating players. Get ready to see your creations move and tell their stories!

5.3. Animation 101: Breathing Life into Your Characters

Now that your characters are visually stunning, it's time to make them move! Animation brings them to life, allowing them to express emotions, interact with the world, and truly tell their story. This section equips you with the fundamental concepts to animate your characters like a pro!

Animation Basics: Building the Blocks

Think of animation as a flipbook on steroids. We create the illusion of movement by displaying a series of slightly different images in rapid succession. Here are the key terms to understand:

- Keyframes: These are the starting and ending poses of an animation sequence.
- In-betweens: Software automatically generates these frames to smoothly transition between keyframes.
- Animation Cycles: Repeated loops of movement, like walk cycles, run cycles, and idle animations.

Mastering the Fundamentals:

Start with these essential animations to build a solid foundation:

- Walk Cycles: Show your character moving at a moderate pace. Focus on natural weight shifting and foot placement.
- Run Cycles: Depict faster movement with exaggerated poses and faster frame rates.
- Idle Animations: Bring life to even static moments with subtle breathing, fidgeting, or glances around.

Emotional Storytelling:

Animation goes beyond just movement – it's about communication. Use animation to convey your character's feelings:

- Facial Expressions: Use blinks, smiles, frowns, and eye movements to express emotions visually.

- Body Language: Slumped posture shows sadness, while puffed-up chest conveys confidence.
- Gestures: Hand gestures and pointing can further emphasize emotions and intentions.

Advanced Moves: Taking It Up a Notch

Once you've mastered the basics, explore more complex actions:

- Jumping and Climbing: Utilize physics simulations or carefully crafted animations for realistic movement.
- Attacking and Defending: Create dynamic combat animations with appropriate impact and reaction.
- Interacting with Objects: Show your character picking up, using, or manipulating objects in the environment.

Pro Tip:

- Use reference videos of real people or animals to observe natural movement patterns.
- Start with simple animations and gradually increase complexity as you gain experience.
- Don't be afraid to experiment – animation is an art form, so let your creativity shine!

Unfortunately, providing actual code snippets for animation is difficult due to the variations in game engine scripting languages and specific workflows.

However, I can offer detailed explanations and illustrative examples to showcase the concepts:

Animation Basics:

- Example (Walk Cycle):
    - Keyframe 1: Character standing with one foot slightly forward.
    - Keyframe 2: Character's weight shifted to the forward foot, other foot raised in mid-step.
    - Keyframe 3: Weight on the other foot, first foot landing.
    - Keyframes 4-6: Repeat with slight variations for a natural walking motion.
    - Software in-betweens the keyframes to create smooth transitions.
- Animation Cycles: Create separate cycles for walking, running, jumping, etc., allowing you to mix and match for diverse movement.

Mastering the Fundamentals:

- Walk Cycle Resources: Utilize online tutorials and motion capture libraries that offer pre-made walk cycles as a starting point.
- Idle Animations: Subtle head tilts, eye blinks, or fidgeting hands can add life to seemingly static moments.

Emotional Storytelling:

- Example (Sadness): Lower head, slumped posture, furrowed brows, slow, downcast eyes.
- Example (Excitement): Wide-eyed expression, open mouth, raised eyebrows, energetic gestures.

Advanced Moves:

- Jumping Animation: Use physics simulations for realistic arc and landing, or hand-animate keyframes for more control.
- Combat Animations: Create separate attack and defense animations for different directions and weapon types.
- Object Interaction: Use inverse kinematics (IK) systems to realistically animate hands reaching for and manipulating objects.

Additional Tips:

- Timing and Spacing: Experiment with the timing and spacing between keyframes to achieve the desired speed and fluidity of movement.
- Overlapping Actions: Overlap animations slightly (e.g., starting the next animation before the previous one finishes) for a more natural look.
- Sound Effects: Add sound effects to enhance the impact and realism of your animations.

Remember, these are just starting points! Animation is a vast and rewarding field, so keep exploring, practicing, and learning new techniques. As you experiment and refine your skills, you'll be able to breathe life into your characters in ever-more expressive and captivating ways.

The next chapter dives into the fascinating world of artificial intelligence (AI) and scripting. Learn how to give your characters minds of their own, allowing them to interact with the world and players in meaningful ways. Get ready to take your character creation journey to the next level!

Chapter 6

Gameplay Mechanics - Let's Go Play!

Buckle up, aspiring game designers, because it's time to delve into the heart of what makes games fun – the mechanics! This chapter equips you with the tools to transform your game world from a pretty backdrop into an interactive playground bursting with movement, challenges, and engaging enemies. Remember, mechanics are the magic that turns pixels into experiences, so let's get started!

6.1. Movement Magic: Guiding Your Hero Through the Game

Imagine your character gliding across meadows, leaping over chasms, or dodging enemy attacks with precision. Movement mechanics are the foundation of how players interact with your world, so let's craft controls that feel intuitive and satisfying.

Mastering the Basics:

- Walk, Run, Jump, Crouch: Implement smooth controls for these essential actions. They're the building blocks of exploration and platforming.
- Advanced Maneuvers: Spice things up with features like sprinting, sliding, or wall-jumping. These cater to specific genres and playstyles.
- Camera Choice: Don't forget the view! Choose fixed angles, top-down perspectives, or dynamic cameras that follow the action.

Pro Tip: Consider physics simulations for realistic movement, especially for jumping and falling. This adds a natural feel to your character's interactions with the environment.

Here are more detailed explanations and illustrative examples to showcase the concepts:

Mastering the Basics:

- Example (Basic Movement in Unity):
    - Use the Input.GetAxis() function to capture WASD key presses.
    - Translate key presses into movement vectors for the character's transform component.
    - Adjust movement speed based on desired walking/running behavior.

- o Implement a jump function with physics forces for realistic jumping arcs.
- Example (Crouching in Unreal Engine):
  - o Define a "Crouch" boolean variable in your character's Blueprint.
  - o Bind a key to a function that sets the "Crouch" variable to true/false.
  - o Adjust the character's capsule collider height and animation state based on the "Crouch" variable.

Advanced Maneuvers:

- Example (Sprinting in Godot):
  - o Implement a double-tap system for the movement keys to trigger a temporary speed boost.
  - o Adjust the character's movement speed and animation state during the sprint duration.
  - o Add visual cues like dust clouds or a stamina bar to indicate sprinting.
- Example (Wall-Jumping in GameMaker Studio 2):
  - o Detect wall collisions using raycasts or specific collision objects.
  - o Apply an impulse force in the opposite direction of the wall upon collision to launch the character upwards.
  - o Limit wall-jumping to specific surfaces or add a cooldown between jumps for balance.

Camera Choice:

- Fixed Cameras: Suitable for 2D platformers or puzzle games where precise positioning is crucial.
- Top-Down Cameras: Offer good overview in isometric or strategy games.
- Dynamic Cameras: Often used in 3D action games, following the character and adjusting dynamically.

Pro Tip: Experiment with different camera angles and movement speeds to find what feels best for your specific game genre and target audience.

Remember, these are just starting points! By understanding the core principles and experimenting with different techniques, you can create movement mechanics that feel both intuitive and engaging for your players.

In the next section, we'll explore how to make your game world truly interactive. Discover how to design puzzles, triggers, and hidden elements that engage players and reward exploration. Get ready to bring your world to life!

6.2. Interactive Objects: Puzzles, Levers, and Breathing Life into Your World

Remember that beautiful landscape you created? It's time to make it sing! Interactive objects are the magic ingredients that transform static scenery into an engaging playground, filled with challenges, secrets, and rewarding moments. Let's explore how to bring your world to life:

Puzzles and Triggers:

- Definition: Puzzles are challenges players must solve using logic, observation, and manipulation of objects. Triggers activate events or changes in the environment when interacted with.
- Examples: Levers that open doors, switches that activate platforms, environmental puzzles that require manipulating objects in specific ways.
- Tips: Design puzzles that are intuitive and challenging but not frustrating. Offer hints or difficulty levels to cater to different players. Use triggers to reward exploration and unlock hidden areas, secrets, or story elements.

Interactive Elements:

- Definition: These are objects that react to player actions, adding depth and engagement to the world.

- Examples: Chests that contain loot, hidden passages leading to new areas, objects that provide information or clues, interactive environmental elements like switches or pressure plates.
- Tips: Consider the purpose of each interactive element. Does it reward exploration, progress the story, or add humor? Make sure interactions feel meaningful and tie into the overall game design.

Environmental Storytelling:

- Definition: Using interactive elements to subtly tell your story without relying solely on dialogue or cutscenes.
- Examples: A broken bridge hinting at a past event, a hidden lever unlocking a secret chamber containing lore, environmental puzzles revealing clues about the game's world or characters.
- Tips: Be creative! Think beyond obvious interactions and use environmental elements to tell your story in unique and engaging ways.

However, here are more detailed explanations and illustrative examples to showcase the concepts:

Puzzles and Triggers:

- Example (Lever Puzzle):

- Place a lever near a locked door. Pulling the lever lowers a bridge across a chasm, allowing passage.
- Use a trigger script attached to the lever that activates the bridge lowering animation when interacted with.
- Add visual cues, like glowing symbols on the lever and bridge, to guide players.
- Example (Environmental Puzzle):
  - Arrange colored pressure plates in a specific sequence to unlock a treasure chest.
  - Use multiple triggers, each detecting a specific color. Only when all correct colors are pressed will the chest unlock trigger activate.
  - Consider adding hints within the environment, like colored markings or murals, to guide players.

Interactive Elements:

- Example (Hidden Passage):
  - Create a secret wall texture that blends seamlessly with the environment.
  - Implement a collision trigger on the hidden wall that teleports the player to a new area when interacted with.

- Add subtle visual cues, like faint cracks or discoloration, to hint at the hidden passage's existence.
- Example (Interactive Object with Information):
  - Place a readable book or inscription on a pedestal.
  - When the player interacts with it, display a text box containing lore, clues, or story elements.
  - Use visual effects like glowing text or a shimmering aura to indicate interactable objects.

Environmental Storytelling:

- Example (Broken Bridge):
  - Design a bridge with missing planks and debris scattered around.
  - Include text etched on nearby rocks hinting at a past battle or natural disaster that destroyed the bridge.
  - This subtly tells a story without explicitly mentioning it in dialogue or cutscenes.
- Example (Secret Chamber):
  - Hide a lever behind a seemingly ordinary painting in a castle hallway.
  - Pulling the lever reveals a hidden door leading to a secret chamber containing treasure or lore scrolls.

○ This rewards exploration and encourages players to interact with their surroundings.

Additional Tips:

- Balance Difficulty: Puzzles and interactive elements should challenge players without being overly frustrating. Consider offering difficulty levels or hints if needed.
- Variety is Key: Use different types of puzzles and interactions to keep the gameplay fresh and engaging.
- Visual Cues: Don't rely solely on text descriptions. Use visual cues like animations, sound effects, and particle effects to guide players and make interactions intuitive.

Remember, these are just starting points! Experiment with different techniques, consider your target audience, and most importantly, have fun creating a world that feels alive and interactive for your players.

In the next section, we'll delve into the exciting world of enemies and combat systems. Learn how to create engaging AI behaviors and mechanics that challenge and thrill your players. Get ready to turn your interactive world into a thrilling adventure!

6.3. Meet Your Match: Creating Enemies and Combat

No hero's journey is complete without challenges! This section equips you with the tools to craft engaging enemies and combat systems that test your players' skills and keep them on the edge of their seats.

Building Basic AI:

Start with simple behaviors to lay the foundation:

- Movement Patterns: Design predictable patrol routes, chase paths, and attack zones for your initial enemies.
- Attack Routines: Implement basic attacks like melee swipes or ranged projectiles.
- Health and Damage: Define health points for enemies and damage values for player attacks.

Level Up Your AI:

As players progress, introduce more complex behaviors:

- Decision-Making: Allow enemies to react to player actions, choose targets, and use cover strategically.
- Flanking Maneuvers: Make enemies smarter by incorporating flanking and coordinated attacks.

- Adaptive Responses: Challenge players further with enemies that adjust their tactics based on the situation.

Crafting Combat Systems:

Tailor your combat to your game's genre and target audience:

- Melee Combat: Design close-quarters action with combos, dodges, and parries.
- Ranged Combat: Implement aiming mechanics, cover systems, and weapon variety.
- Special Abilities: Add unique skills for both players and enemies to spice up combat encounters.

Remember:

- Start Simple: Introduce basic enemies and mechanics first, gradually increasing complexity as players gain experience.
- Balance is Key: Ensure combat feels fair and challenging, not frustrating. Playtest and adjust difficulty accordingly.
- Variety is Thrilling: Offer different enemy types, abilities, and environments to keep combat fresh and engaging.

However, I can offer detailed explanations and illustrative examples to showcase the concepts:

Building Basic AI:

- Example (Patrol Enemy):
  - Define waypoints along a set path for the enemy to move between.
  - Use a script to move the enemy towards the current waypoint and update the target waypoint when reached.
  - Add a detection range and trigger an attack function if the player enters it.
- Example (Basic Attack):
  - Create an animation for the enemy's attack.
  - Use a trigger collider on the enemy's weapon that deals damage to the player when overlapped during the attack animation.
  - Reduce the player's health based on the enemy's attack damage.

Level Up Your AI:

- Example (Decision-Making):
  - Implement a health threshold that triggers a defensive behavior (retreating) when enemy health falls below a certain level.
  - Alternatively, prioritize attacking the player with the lowest health for strategic targeting.
- Example (Flanking Maneuvers):

- During combat, have the enemy move around the player to try and attack from the side or back.
- This adds complexity and forces players to be aware of their surroundings.
- Example (Adaptive Responses):
  - If the player frequently dodges a specific attack, have the enemy switch to a different attack pattern.
  - This keeps combat dynamic and forces players to adapt their tactics.

Crafting Combat Systems:

- Example (Melee Combat):
  - Implement light and heavy attacks with different animations and damage values.
  - Allow players to dodge or parry enemy attacks based on timing and input.
  - Add combos by chaining different attacks together for increased damage.
- Example (Ranged Combat):
  - Design a crosshair aiming system for precise targeting.
  - Implement cover mechanics where players can take cover behind objects to reduce damage.
  - Include different weapon types with varying firing rates, damage, and reload times.

- Example (Special Abilities):
  - Give the player a shield ability to block enemy attacks temporarily.
  - Design an enemy spellcaster that throws fireballs or creates area-of-effect damage zones.
  - Special abilities add variety and strategic depth to combat encounters.

Remember:

- Experiment with different behaviors and mechanics to find what works best for your game's style and genre.
- Utilize visual cues and sound effects to communicate enemy intentions and attack timing clearly to players.
- Playtest extensively and gather feedback to fine-tune difficulty, balance, and overall combat experience.

By understanding these core concepts and experimenting with various approaches, you can craft engaging enemies and combat systems that challenge and thrill your players, pushing them to their limits and making their victories all the more rewarding.

This is just the beginning of your gameplay mechanics journey! In the next chapter, we'll explore advanced topics like inventory systems, level design, and user interfaces, taking your game's interactivity and engagement to the next level.

Are you ready to turn your mechanics into unforgettable player experiences? Turn the page, adventurer, and let's continue building your dream game together!

Part 3: Polishing Your Gem and Sharing Your Creation

Chapter 7

Optimization: Making Your Game Shine on Any Device

Congratulations, you've built an amazing game! But before you share your masterpiece with the world, let's ensure it runs smoothly on any device, from high-end PCs to budget phones. This chapter equips you with the knowledge to optimize your game and deliver a stellar experience for every player.

7.1. Performance Boosters: Tools and Techniques for Smoother Gameplay

Imagine your players diving into your game, only to be met with choppy frame rates and sluggish controls. No bueno! This section equips you with the tools and techniques to optimize your game and deliver a silky-smooth, lag-free experience on any device.

Profiling and Analysis:

Before diving in blindly, identify the culprits! Use profiling tools built into your game engine to pinpoint performance bottlenecks. These tools analyze various aspects like CPU usage, GPU usage, and memory allocation, highlighting areas that need optimization love. Focus on areas with high spikes or sustained usage that could be impacting gameplay smoothness.

Smart Simplification:

Sometimes, less is more! While stunning visuals are great, don't sacrifice performance at the altar of complexity. Here are some optimization techniques:

- Model Optimization: Simplify 3D models by reducing polygon count or using techniques like level of detail (LOD) to swap in less detailed versions as objects move further away from the camera.
- Texture Tweaks: Reduce texture resolution for less critical elements or utilize texture atlases to pack multiple textures into a single file,

minimizing texture switches and improving texture fetching efficiency.

- Animation Efficiency: Analyze animations and remove unnecessary frames or simplify complex movements. Remember, smooth gameplay often trumps hyper-realistic animation every time.

Level of Detail (LOD):

This is a magic trick for maintaining visual quality while optimizing performance. Implement LOD systems that swap detailed objects for simpler, less resource-intensive versions as they move farther away from the camera. This ensures smooth visuals across various viewing distances without sacrificing frame rate.

Caching with Care:

Pre-loading essential assets like textures, animations, and levels into memory can significantly reduce loading times and stuttering. This is like preparing a delicious meal beforehand – your players get to dig right in without waiting! But be mindful not to overload memory with unnecessary assets. Strike a balance between fast loading and efficient memory usage.

Here are more detailed explanations and illustrative examples to showcase the concepts:

Profiling and Analysis:

- Example: Imagine your game runs smoothly on your powerful computer, but stutters on older laptops. Use profiling tools to see if the GPU usage spikes during specific scenes with complex models and textures. This identifies the area for optimization.

Smart Simplification:

- Example (Model Optimization): In a racing game, use highly detailed models for cars close to the player, but switch to simpler versions for distant cars. This reduces polygon count without sacrificing the overall racing experience.

- Example (Texture Tweaks): Instead of using a 4096x4096 texture for a distant mountain, use a smaller 512x512 version. You can still achieve a visually pleasing mountain while saving memory and improving texture fetching speed.

Level of Detail (LOD):

- Example: In an open-world RPG, use a detailed character model when the player is close, but switch to a simpler version with less detail when they're far away. This maintains visual quality when exploring vast landscapes without impacting performance.

Caching with Care:

- Example: Pre-load the textures and animations for the next level before the player enters it. This eliminates loading screens and ensures a seamless transition, keeping the player immersed in the game.

Additional Tips:

- Utilize batching: Combine similar objects (e.g., trees) into a single draw call to reduce rendering overhead.
- Optimize shaders: Complex shaders can be beautiful, but simpler ones run faster. Consider adjusting them for specific rendering needs.
- Enable compression: Compress textures and audio files to reduce their size without sacrificing quality significantly.

Remember: The key to effective optimization is finding the right balance between visual fidelity and performance. Experiment, test on various devices, and gather player feedback to find the sweet spot for your game.

By following these tips and continuously profiling and analyzing your game, you can ensure a smooth and enjoyable experience for all your players.

7.2. Memory Management: Keeping Your Game Light on Its Feet

Imagine your game running slow, bogged down by forgotten objects. Yikes! This section equips you with memory management skills to keep your game lean and mean, ensuring a smooth experience for all players.

Cleaning Up After Yourself:

Just like cleaning your room, your game needs tidying up too! When objects or data are no longer needed, get rid of them using your engine's specific commands. Think of it as recycling – good for the environment (your game's memory) and good for performance!

Beware of Memory Hogs:

Big textures, hefty audio files, and complex models are like memory monsters. Be mindful of their file size and impact on memory usage. Consider alternative, lighter-weight options or optimization techniques to keep your game trim and fit.

Object Pooling: Rent, Don't Buy:

Imagine reusing plates at a party instead of creating new ones each time. Object pooling does the same! Instead of creating new objects all the time, reuse commonly used ones, reducing memory allocation and keeping things tidy. It's like having a pool of rental objects, ready to be used and reused efficiently.

Remember: Memory management is an ongoing task. Regularly check your game's memory usage and address any leaks you find. Think of it as keeping your game healthy and fit for smooth gameplay.

In the next section, we'll explore optimizing for mobile devices, making your game shine even on the smallest screens. Get ready to conquer the pocket-sized gaming world!

By following these tips and keeping your game lean and mean, you'll ensure a happy player experience, free from lag and frustration. Happy optimizing!

7.3. Pocket Powerhouses: Optimizing for Mobile Devices

Mobile devices are the ultimate gaming companions, offering fun on the go. But their smaller size and processing power demand special attention. This section equips you with the knowledge to optimize your game for mobile devices, ensuring a seamless and enjoyable experience for your pocket-sized players.

Intuitive Controls: Touch-Friendly Fun:

Ditch the complex keyboard and mouse controls! Design intuitive touch controls or simple virtual joysticks that are comfortable and responsive on touchscreens. Imagine your players tapping, swiping, and tilting their devices with ease, immersed in the game's world.

Visual Fidelity vs. Performance:

Mobile devices have limitations, so striking a balance is key. Consider offering scaled-down graphics settings or options for lower-end devices. Remember, smooth gameplay often trumps hyper-realistic visuals when it comes to mobile gaming satisfaction.

Battery Buddies: Saving Power for Longer Play:

Nobody wants a game that drains their battery in minutes! Implement features like screen dimming or frame rate reduction during inactivity to conserve precious battery life. Imagine your players enjoying extended gaming sessions without worrying about their phone dying mid-adventure.

Touch Feedback: Bringing Immersion to Fingertips:

Subtle vibrations or sound effects can enhance touch interactions, making your game feel more responsive and engaging. Imagine players feeling the impact of their attacks or the rumble of the ground during intense moments, adding another layer of immersion to their mobile experience.

Here are more detailed explanations and illustrative examples to showcase the concepts:

Intuitive Controls:

- Example: In a platformer, use virtual buttons for jumping and movement, placed at comfortable positions on the screen. Consider context-sensitive controls that change depending on the situation (e.g., swiping for a quick attack, holding for a charged attack).
- Example: In a puzzle game, utilize touch gestures like taps, drags, and pinches to manipulate objects or rotate the camera. Ensure controls are responsive and provide clear visual feedback for player actions.

Visual Fidelity vs. Performance:

- Example: Offer adjustable graphics settings like texture quality, shadow detail, and anti-aliasing. Allow players to find the balance between visual fidelity and smooth performance based on their device capabilities.
- Example: Use techniques like texture atlases and model simplification to reduce memory usage without sacrificing too much visual quality.

Remember, mobile players often prioritize smooth gameplay over ultra-realistic graphics.

Battery Buddies:

- Example: Implement an "auto-adjust graphics" option that automatically scales down settings based on battery level or device temperature to conserve power.
- Example: Allow players to set frame rate caps or enable battery saver mode, giving them control over their device's power consumption during gameplay.

Touch Feedback:

- Example: Add subtle vibrations for button presses, weapon impacts, or character movements. Use sound effects that complement the vibrations to create a more immersive touch experience.
- Example: Implement haptic feedback for specific events in the game, like explosions, puzzle successes, or character damage. This provides tactile feedback that enhances player engagement.

Additional Tips:

- Optimize loading times: Utilize asset loading techniques like background loading and compressed assets to minimize wait times.
- Test on various devices: Ensure your game performs well on a range of devices with different processing power and screen sizes.
- Gather player feedback: Ask players about their experience and preferences to identify areas for improvement in mobile optimization.

Remember: Mobile optimization is about striking a balance between features, visuals, and performance. Experiment, test, and gather feedback to create a game that is enjoyable, engaging, and runs smoothly on any mobile device, leaving your players wanting more!

By following these tips and prioritizing a smooth, engaging experience, you can turn your game into a mobile masterpiece, conquering the hearts (and pockets) of players everywhere!

In the next chapter, we'll delve into the exciting world of user interfaces (UI) and user experience (UX), crafting interfaces that are not only functional but also intuitive and enjoyable to use. Get ready to make your game truly user-friendly and captivating!

Chapter 8

Sharing Your Masterpiece - Packaging and Exporting Your Game

Congratulations, you've poured your heart and soul into crafting a game! But your journey isn't over yet. It's time to unleash your creation upon the world, to share the joy you've poured into every line of code, every pixel, every meticulously crafted level. This chapter equips you with the tools and knowledge to navigate the exciting (and sometimes baffling) world of packaging, exporting, and distribution. Buckle up, because it's time to turn your game into a global phenomenon!

8.1. Platform Powerhouse: Exporting Your Game Like a Pro

So you've crafted a game that rocks! Now it's time to unleash it on the world, but each platform has its own key. This section equips you with those keys, unlocking doors to desktops, mobiles, and even beyond!

Desktop Domination:

- Windows, Mac, Linux: Master the art of exporting for different systems. We'll cover tools, formats, and make your game run smoothly on diverse setups. Imagine your masterpiece on countless PC screens!
- Mobile Mastery: Conquer the pocket-sized powerhouses: iOS and Android. Explore app store requirements, optimization tricks, and captivating mobile players. Picture your game enjoyed on commutes, breaks, and everywhere in between!

Beyond the Obvious:

- Consoles, Web, VR: Dream bigger! We'll explore exporting for consoles, web platforms, and even virtual reality headsets. Imagine seeing your game on the big screen or transporting players to immersive VR worlds!

Her are more detailed explanations and illustrative examples to solidify the concepts:

Desktop Domination:

- Example (Windows): Utilize tools like Unity's Build Settings or Unreal Engine's Packaging system to export an executable file (.exe) compatible with Windows systems. Configure settings like target architecture (32-bit or 64-bit) and prerequisites (e.g., DirectX libraries) for smooth installation and play.

- Example (Mac): Use tools like Unity's Xcode Export or Unreal Engine's Mac Build option to generate a macOS application bundle (.app). Ensure proper code signing and notarization for Apple's gatekeeper security checks.

- Example (Linux): Utilize platform-specific tools and libraries (e.g., SDL, GLFW) to create a single executable or distribute the game as source code for compilation on various Linux distributions. Consider offering different build options for 32-bit and 64-bit architectures.

Mobile Mastery:

- Example (iOS): Follow Apple's App Store guidelines and Xcode instructions for exporting your game as an iOS app (.ipa file). This involves code signing, provisioning profiles, and adhering to specific technical requirements.

- Example (Android): Utilize Android Studio or Unity's Android Build Settings to generate an Android App Bundle (.aab) or an APK file. Consider offering multiple APK variants for different device configurations and screen resolutions.

- Example (Mobile Optimization): Reduce texture sizes, simplify 3D models, and utilize efficient shaders to ensure smooth performance on mobile devices with varying processing power.

Beyond the Obvious:

- Example (Consoles): Partner with publishers or middleware providers to navigate the complex console submission processes, including specific development kits, certification requirements, and content guidelines.
- Example (Web Platforms): Utilize web technologies like WebGL or HTML5 Canvas to create browser-based versions of your game. Consider cloud gaming platforms for high-end graphics and broader reach.
- Example (VR): Explore development tools and platforms specific to VR headsets (e.g., Oculus SDK, SteamVR) to create immersive experiences that leverage headset features and motion controls.

Remember: Experiment, research, and consult platform-specific documentation for the most up-to-date export requirements and best practices. By understanding the nuances of each platform, you can ensure your game reaches players seamlessly and delivers an enjoyable experience regardless of where they choose to play.

Bonus Tip: Utilize online communities and forums to connect with other developers and share knowledge about exporting and optimizing for different platforms!

8.2. Unleashing Your Game: Finding Your Audience on Shelves (Digital and Real)

You've honed your game to perfection, but how do you get it into players' hands? This section equips you with the know-how to navigate the exciting world of distribution channels:

Digital Storefronts:

- Steam, itch.io, App Store, Google Play: These online marketplaces are your virtual shelves. We'll break down submission processes, pricing strategies, and stand out in a crowded field. Imagine your game listed alongside industry giants!
- Key Partners: Consider teaming up with publishers or distributors for wider reach and marketing muscle. We'll discuss partnership models, negotiation tips, and finding the right fit for your game. Picture industry veterans amplifying your voice!

Building Your Community:

- Don't underestimate the power of fans! We'll show you how to foster an engaged community, gather feedback, and create a space where players feel valued. Imagine a passionate community cheering you on!

However, here are more detailed examples and practical insights:

Digital Storefronts:

- Steam:
    - Create a Steamworks account and follow submission guidelines, including providing game descriptions, screenshots, trailers, and setting pricing.
    - Consider Early Access for feedback and funding during development.
    - Utilize Steam's marketing tools like sales, events, and visibility features.
- itch.io:
    - Set up a developer page and upload your game easily, customizing store pages and setting flexible pricing models (pay-what-you-want, demos, bundles).
    - Engage with the indie dev community for feedback and support.
- App Store and Google Play:

- Register as a developer, adhere to specific guidelines for app content and format, and manage pricing and in-app purchases.
- Optimize app store listings with keywords and visuals for discoverability.

Key Partners:

- Publishers:
  - Research publishers who align with your game's genre and audience.
  - Understand different partnership models (funding, marketing, distribution support).
  - Negotiate terms carefully, considering revenue splits, intellectual property rights, and creative control.
- Distributors:
  - Partner with distributors who offer specialized services like physical retail distribution or localization for specific regions.

Building Your Community:

- Social Media: Create engaging content on platforms like Twitter, Facebook, and Discord to connect with players, share updates, and build excitement.

- Forums and Subreddits: Participate in relevant communities, answer questions, and gather feedback to foster a sense of belonging and ownership among fans.
- Early Access or Beta Testing: Invite players to test early versions, providing valuable feedback and building a core community of early adopters.

Remember: Experiment with different channels and strategies to find what works best for your game and audience. Continuously evaluate and adjust your approach to maximize reach and engagement.

Pro Tip: Research each platform's audience and trends to understand where your game will resonate most.

8.3. Sound the Hype! Marketing and Building a Fanatical Community

Your game is polished, your distribution channels are set, but how do you ignite the spark that turns players into raving fans? This section equips you with the tools to craft a captivating message, build a vibrant community, and leverage data to make informed decisions.

Crafting Your Message:

- Know Your Audience: Who are you trying to reach? What are their interests and gaming habits? Tailor your message to resonate with their desires and expectations. Imagine crafting trailers and descriptions that speak directly to their hearts (and thumbs)!

- Stand Out from the Crowd: A crowded marketplace demands a unique voice. Highlight your game's distinct features, story, or gameplay mechanics. Picture your game being the eye-catching gem amidst a sea of titles!
- Press & Influencers: Partner with relevant media outlets and gaming influencers to spread the word. Provide exclusive content, early access, or interviews to generate buzz and reach new audiences. Imagine your game being featured in articles, videos, and streams, watched by thousands of potential players!

Community Cultivation:

- Foster Two-Way Communication: Respond to comments, answer questions, and actively engage with your community. Show players you care and value their feedback. Imagine a thriving online space where players feel heard and appreciated!
- Create Meaningful Interactions: Host contests, organize events, or offer exclusive rewards to keep your community engaged. Encourage players to share their experiences and connect with each other. Picture a vibrant community buzzing with excitement and shared passion for your game!

- Listen & Adapt: Pay close attention to feedback and suggestions. Use it to improve your game, add new features, and cater to your community's evolving needs. Imagine your game constantly evolving based on the collective voice of your fans!

Data-Driven Decisions:

- Track Key Metrics: Analyze website traffic, social media engagement, and player behavior to understand what resonates with your audience. Use this data to inform future marketing efforts and community initiatives. Imagine making strategic decisions based on real-world data, not just guesses!
- Experiment & Iterate: Don't be afraid to try new things! Test different marketing strategies, community events, and content formats to see what works best. Adapt and refine your approach based on the data you gather. Picture constantly optimizing your efforts for maximum impact!

However, here are more detailed examples and practical insights:

Crafting Your Message:

- Target Audience: Identify your game's genre, themes, and mechanics, then research demographics and interests of those who enjoy similar games.

- Unique Selling Points: Highlight what makes your game stand out, whether it's innovative gameplay, compelling characters, or a captivating story.
- Press Releases: Craft well-written press releases outlining key features, target platforms, release date, and contact information.
- Social Media Presence: Create engaging content across platforms like Twitter, Facebook, Instagram, and Discord, tailored to each platform's audience and style.
- Trailers and Screenshots: Showcase your game's visuals and gameplay with high-quality trailers and screenshots, capturing attention and excitement.

Community Building:

- Social Media Groups: Establish official communities on Facebook, Discord, or Reddit for discussion, feedback, and announcements.
- Forums: Create a dedicated forum on your website for in-depth discussions, bug reports, and suggestions.
- Livestreams and Events: Host developer livestreams to showcase gameplay, answer questions, and interact directly with fans.
- Contests and Giveaways: Generate excitement and engagement through contests, giveaways, or early access opportunities.

- User-Generated Content: Encourage fans to create and share content like fanart, gameplay videos, or reviews to promote your game organically.

Data-Driven Decisions:

- Website Analytics: Track website traffic, page views, bounce rates, and popular content to understand user behavior and interests.
- Social Media Insights: Analyze engagement metrics (likes, shares, comments) to identify what resonates with your audience and refine your content strategy.
- Player Feedback: Gather feedback through surveys, forums, or social media polls to understand player preferences and identify areas for improvement.

Note: Marketing and community building are ongoing processes that evolve alongside your game and its audience. Continuously experiment, adapt, and learn to create a thriving community of passionate fans who support your game's success.

Remember: Marketing and community building are marathons, not sprints. Be patient, consistent, and adaptable. By understanding your audience, crafting a compelling message, and fostering a thriving community, you can turn players into loyal fans who champion your game and fuel its success. So, crank up the hype, engage your audience, and get ready to witness the power of a passionate community!

Chapter 9

Level Up! Resources and Beyond

Congratulations, you've conquered the basics of game development! Now it's time to push your skills to the next level, explore new horizons, and become the ultimate gamedev legend. This chapter equips you with the tools and knowledge to keep learning, growing, and creating ever-more awesome games. Buckle up, adventurer, because the journey never ends!

9.1. Indie Dev Spotlight: Unveiling the Secrets of Success

The indie game scene isn't just a breeding ground for innovation; it's a treasure trove of knowledge waiting to be unearthed. In this section, we'll shine a light on the journeys of successful indie developers, dissecting their triumphs and challenges to glean valuable lessons applicable to everyone, from aspiring devs to seasoned veterans.

Learning from the Masters:

- Indie Dev Interviews: Imagine sitting down with the creators of your favorite indie hits! Dive deep into their development processes, marketing strategies, and the stories behind their game-changing ideas through insightful interviews. Learn from their successes, and most importantly, their stumbles, to gain a well-rounded perspective on the indie dev journey.
- Postmortems and Case Studies: Not every project reaches the finish line, but even failures hold valuable lessons. Analyze real-world projects through detailed postmortems and case studies. Learn what worked, what didn't, and how common pitfalls were navigated. Consider these as cautionary tales and roadmaps to success rolled into one!
- Community Forums and Groups: The indie dev community thrives on sharing and collaboration. Tap into this wealth of knowledge by joining online forums and groups. Connect with other developers, share experiences, ask questions, and learn from the collective wisdom of a passionate community. Remember, you're not alone in this!

Here are more specific examples of resources and insights:

Examples of Indie Dev Interviews:

- Celeste Postmortem: <invalid URL removed>
- Stardew Valley Interview: <invalid URL removed>
- Hollow Knight Interview: <invalid URL removed>

Examples of Postmortems and Case Studies:

- Hyper Light Drifter Postmortem: <invalid URL removed>
- No Man's Sky Case Study: <invalid URL removed>
- Cuphead's Development Story: <invalid URL removed>

Examples of Community Forums and Groups:

- Unity Forums: https://forum.unity.com/
- GameDev.net Forums: https://www.gamedev.net/forums/
- Indie Game Developers Reddit: https://www.reddit.com/r/IndieGaming/
- Indie Game Developers on Facebook: <invalid URL removed>

Additional Tips:

- Seek out interviews and postmortems related to your game genre or desired platforms.
- Join communities that align with your interests and development tools.

- Don't be afraid to ask questions and engage in discussions.
- Share your own experiences and insights to contribute to the community's knowledge base.
- Follow successful indie devs on social media to stay updated on their projects and advice.

Remember: The indie dev community is your support system and learning ground. By actively engaging with these resources, you'll not only gain knowledge but also discover the inspiration and encouragement to create your own success story. But the learning doesn't stop there...

Key Terms:

- Indie Dev: An independent game developer, typically creating games outside of large studios.
- Postmortem: An analysis of a completed project, focusing on both successes and failures.
- Case Study: An in-depth examination of a specific project, highlighting key decisions, challenges, and outcomes.

Pro Tip: Look for communities specific to your game genre or development tools for even more targeted learning and support!

9.2. Level Up Your Skills: A Treasure Trove of Online Resources

The internet is a game developer's playground, bursting with resources to hone your craft. This section equips you with the best tools to quench your knowledge thirst, from beginner-friendly guides to advanced masterclasses. Get ready to supercharge your skills and push your creative boundaries!

Tutorial Time:

- Dive into Online Courses: Explore a universe of online tutorials and courses designed for every skill level. Master new programming languages, design principles, or storytelling techniques at your own pace. Imagine crafting intricate mechanics, weaving captivating narratives, or coding like a pro – the possibilities are endless!
- Unlock Official Docs and Wikis: Unleash the full potential of your chosen game engine or development tools by delving into official documentation and community-driven wikis. Uncover hidden features, troubleshoot issues, and become an expert in your toolkit. Picture yourself wielding your tools with ninja-like precision!
- Stay Informed with Blogs and Articles: Stay ahead of the curve with industry blogs and articles covering the latest trends, technologies, and insights. Absorb wisdom from experienced

developers, discover cutting-edge tools, and keep your finger on the ever-evolving gamedev pulse. Imagine being an innovation guru, ready to tackle any challenge the industry throws your way!

Here are more specific examples of resources and insights:

Examples of Online Courses:

- Unity Learn: Official tutorials and courses for Unity game engine (https://learn.unity.com/)
- Unreal Engine Online Learning: Courses for Unreal Engine (<invalid URL removed>)
- Coursera: Offers game development courses from universities and studios (https://www.coursera.org/courses?query=game%20development)
- Udemy: Wide range of game development courses (<invalid URL removed>)
- Codecademy: Interactive courses for programming languages (https://www.codecademy.com/)

Examples of Documentation and Wikis:

- Unity Documentation: Comprehensive documentation for Unity (https://docs.unity3d.com/Manual/index.html)
- Unreal Engine Documentation: Official Unreal Engine documentation (https://docs.unrealengine.com/en-US/)

- GameDev.net Wiki: Community-driven wiki covering various game development topics (<invalid URL removed>)

Examples of Blogs and Articles:

- Game Developer Magazine: Industry insights and tutorials (https://www.gdmag.com/)
- Unity Blog: Official Unity blog with news and best practices (https://blog.unity.com/)
- Gamasutra: Articles on game design, development, and business (https://www.gamasutra.com/)
- 8o.lv: Technical art and game development articles (https://8o.lv/)

Pro Tip: Combine resources! Use tutorials to learn new skills, then consult documentation for specifics, and stay updated with blogs for industry trends.

Key Terms:

- Online Courses: Structured learning platforms offering video lectures, quizzes, and projects.
- Documentation: Official guides and instructions for specific tools or software.
- Wikis: Collaborative online repositories of information, often community-driven.
- Blogs and Articles: Regularly updated content covering industry news, insights, and tutorials.

Ready to explore further? In the next section, we'll delve into advanced topics to truly push your creative boundaries and solidify your place as a gamedev extraordinaire!

9.3. Beyond the Basics: Expanding Your Game Dev Horizons

Feeling like a gamedev master in the making? This section is your launchpad to even more exciting challenges. We'll explore advanced topics and areas to push your boundaries and solidify your place as a game-crafting legend!

Genre Bending:

- Step Outside Your Comfort Zone: Don't limit yourself! Explore new genres – design a mind-bending puzzle, craft a captivating narrative adventure, or dive into the world of multiplayer experiences. Imagine creating games that surprise even yourself, discovering hidden talents, and expanding your creative horizons!

Programming Prowess:

- Master the Code: Delve into complex programming concepts like algorithms, data structures, and optimization techniques. These skills unlock doors to crafting more efficient, performant, and technically impressive games. Picture yourself writing code that's not just functional, but elegant and efficient, like a programming ninja!

Design Deep Dive:

- Go Beyond the Surface: Explore advanced game design principles like player psychology, level design theory, and storytelling techniques. Refine your ability to craft engaging experiences that truly resonate with players. Imagine designing games that not only look good, but captivate players for hours on end, leaving them wanting more!

Here are more detailed examples and resources for each advanced topic:

Genre Exploration:

- Puzzle Games: Explore logic-based challenges and spatial reasoning through games like Tetris, Portal, or The Witness.
- Narrative Adventures: Craft immersive stories and player choices in games like Life is Strange, The Walking Dead, or Firewatch.
- Multiplayer Experiences: Create social interactions and competitive gameplay in games like Among Us, Overwatch, or Rocket League.

Programming Mastery:

- Algorithms:
  - Pathfinding: Implement A* search for efficient character navigation (examples in Unity tutorials).
  - Collision Detection: Use bounding boxes or quadtrees for accurate collision checks (examples in Unreal Engine documentation).
- Data Structures:
  - Arrays and Lists: Store and manage game objects and data efficiently (examples in C# or Python tutorials).
  - Trees: Organize hierarchical structures like game menus or levels (examples in C++ or Java tutorials).
- Optimization:
  - Profiling Tools: Identify performance bottlenecks in your code (Unity Profiler, Unreal Engine Insights).
  - Caching Techniques: Store frequently used data for faster retrieval (examples in game development articles).
  - Level of Detail (LOD): Adjust model complexity based on distance (examples in game engine documentation).

Design Deep Dive:

- Player Psychology:

- Motivation: Understand intrinsic and extrinsic motivators to keep players engaged (examples in game design books like "The Art of Game Design" by Jesse Schell).
- Flow State: Create a balance between challenge and skill to foster immersion (examples in articles on game flow).
- Level Design Theory:
  - Pacing and Challenge: Craft varied levels with balanced difficulty curves (examples in level design tutorials).
  - Visual Communication: Guide players through environmental cues and visual storytelling (examples in game art and design books).
- Storytelling Techniques:
  - Narrative Structure: Use plot devices and character arcs to create compelling stories (examples in screenwriting resources).
  - Environmental Storytelling: Show, don't tell, by embedding narrative elements in the game world (examples in games like Gone Home or Bioshock).

Remember: The possibilities in game development are endless. This section is just a starting point for your continued exploration and growth. So, keep learning, keep creating, and keep pushing the boundaries of what's possible. The exciting world of game development awaits!

Key Terms:

- Genre: A category of games with similar characteristics, like puzzle, adventure, or multiplayer.
- Algorithm: A set of instructions for solving a problem or completing a task.
- Data Structure: A way of organizing and storing data for efficient access and manipulation.
- Optimization: Techniques to improve the performance of a game, making it run smoother and faster.

Pro Tip: Look for communities or forums specifically focused on your areas of interest, like advanced programming or specific game genres. This allows you to connect with like-minded developers and learn from their expertise!

Next up: We'll wrap up this guide with some parting words of wisdom and encouragement to fuel your journey as a game developer. Don't miss it!

Wrapping Up: Your Game Dev Odyssey Begins Now!

Phew! We've traversed the exciting landscape of game development, from the fundamentals of coding and design to the vast open plains of exploration and experimentation. Remember, this is just the beginning of your incredible journey. Think of this book as your trusty map, guiding you through the initial stages, but the real adventure lies beyond the final page.

Remember: Game development is a marathon, not a sprint. Embrace the challenges, celebrate the victories, and most importantly, never stop learning and growing. The more you delve into this amazing world, the more you'll discover its depth and potential. It's a journey of self-expression, pushing boundaries, and creating something truly magical that can touch the lives of others.

So, what are you waiting for? Dust off your keyboard, fire up your game engine, and let your creativity take flight! The world needs your unique games, your innovative ideas, and your passion for this incredible art form.

Remember, every legendary game developer started somewhere, and that somewhere is right here, right now.

But wait, there's more! In the bonus section, we'll equip you with additional resources, tools, and inspirational stories to fuel your game development journey. Consider it your secret weapon pack, ready to be unleashed as you embark on your epic quest to become a game-crafting legend! Don't miss it!

Now, go forth, young developer, and create something amazing! The world awaits your masterpiece.

www.ingramcontent.com/pod-product-compliance
Lightning Source LLC
LaVergne TN
LVHW051737050326
832903LV00023B/963